The Creation-Evolution Debate

George H. Shriver
Lecture Series
in Religion
in American History
No. 3

THE CREATION-EVOLUTION DEBATE

Historical Perspectives

Edward J. Larson

The University of Georgia Press
Athens & London

© 2007 by the University of Georgia Press
Athens, Georgia 30602
All rights reserved

Set in 10/16 Aldus
Printed and bound by Thomson-Shore
The paper in this book meets the guidelines for permanence
and durability of the Committee on Production Guidelines
for Book Longevity of the Council on Library Resources.

Printed in the United States of America

07 08 09 10 11 C 5 4 3 2 1

Library of Congress Cataloging-in-Publication Data

Larson, Edward J. (Edward John)
The creation-evolution debate : historical perspectives /
Edward J. Larson.
p. cm. — (George H. Shriver lecture series in
religion in American history ; no. 3)
Includes index.
ISBN-13: 978-0-8203-2912-3 (hardcover : alk. paper)
ISBN-10: 0-8203-2912-6 (hardcover : alk. paper)
1. Evolution (Biology) — Religious aspects — Christianity.
2. Evolution (Biology) — United States. 3. Creationism — United
States. 4. Religion and science — United States. 5. Scientists —
United States. 6. Scientists — Religious life. I. Title.
BL263.L32 2007
231.7'6520973 — dc22   2006018989

British Library Cataloging-in-Publication Data available

To David C. Lindberg

*an extraordinary teacher
and modern pioneer in the history
of science and religion*

CONTENTS

FOREWORD

The material in this volume derives from the 2006 George L. Shriver Lectures: Religion in American History, presented at Stetson University on January 24 and 25. The Shriver Lectures were established by Dr. George Shriver, a Stetson alumnus, to bring noted scholars to the university to speak about the influence and significance of religion in the history and development of American society. George Shriver, himself a historian of religion, spent the major part of his career in the history department at Georgia Southern University, where he won awards for both his teaching and his research. Professor Shriver's generous gifts to the university endowed this lectureship and provided for the publication of the lectures. Jointly sponsored by the Department of Religious Studies and the Department of History at Stetson, these lectures combine two of George Shriver's scholarly passions — religious studies and history.

The 2006 lectures were delivered by Dr. Edward J. Larson, Talmadge Chair of Law and Russell Professor of American History at the University of Georgia. An insightful author and engaging speaker, Professor Larson has authored six books and more than sixty published articles, dealing with topics related to legal history, law, and bioethics. Two of his books have dealt specifically with the topic of his Shriver Lectures. His first book, *Trial and Error: The American Controversy over Creation and Evolution* (1985, expanded editions 1989 and 2002), chronicled the legal battles over teaching evolution in American public schools. In 1997 he published *Summer of the Gods: The Scopes Trial and America's Continuing Debate over Science and Religion,* for which he won the 1998 Pulitzer Prize in History.

The topic of Professor Larson's lectures is important because of the role of the evolution debate in America's past, but it is also timely because of the continued controversy over the teaching of evolution in public schools. The conflict between evolution and "intelligent design" has become an especially volatile issue in recent years, sometimes dividing school boards, communities, and even legislatures. In his first lecture, Larson provides a historical review of the development of and initial reaction to Charles Darwin's theory of evolution. He demonstrates that the strongest objections to Darwin's views focused on the idea that humans evolved from lower primates, because a naturalistic human evolution seemed to leave no room for humankind's spiritual side. The most famous (and carnivalesque) battle between religion and evolution took place in Dayton, Tennessee, the venue for the Scopes trial in 1925. This trial, along with events preceding and following it, is the subject of Larson's second lecture. In his third and final lecture, Professor Larson examines the attitudes of scientists toward religion, focusing particularly on the American scientific community.

Deepest appreciation is expressed to George Shriver for his generosity in funding this lectureship and his continued interest in scholarly inquiry and the dissemination of learning. His commitment to critical inquiry, informed reflection, and public discourse represents the highest ideals of the teaching scholar. I would also like to thank Ed Larson, not only for his engaging and insightful lectures, but also for his generous spirit during his visit to our campus. Gratitude must also be expressed to the following: Dr. H. Douglas Lee, president of Stetson University, and his wife Margaret, who served as gracious hosts for a Shriver dinner and have been supportive of the Shriver Lectures since their inception; Professor Kevin O'Keefe, of Stetson's Department of History, who helped plan and implement the lectures; the editors and staff of the University of Georgia Press for their excellent job in publishing the Shriver Lecture Series; and especially Lisa Guenther, administrative specialist for the Department of Religious Studies, whose careful attention to the numerous details of the lectureship contributed enormously to the success of the lectures.

Mitchell G. Reddish, Chair
George H. Shriver Lectures Committee
Stetson University

PREFACE

In his role as chair of the George H. Shriver Lectures Committee at Stetson University, Mitchell G. Reddish asked me to speak on the history science and religion in America, with particular reference to the continuing debate over the teaching of evolution in public schools. At the time of his invitation, this debate had intensified with the revival of popular interest, especially among American Evangelicals, in the doctrines of Intelligent Design as an alternative to the theory of organic evolution for explaining life's diversity. I responded with a series of three lectures delivered in January 2006 on the Stetson University campus in DeLand, Florida. My audience included Stetson faculty and students as well as hundreds of people from the surrounding community.

In preparing my lectures for delivery and publication, I used as my model an earlier series of Shriver Lectures by America's premiere historian of religion, Martin E. Marty. In the preface to his published lectures, Marty discussed the challenge of turning spoken lectures into a printed book. His wise words are worth repeating here because they apply to this work as well as his own. "We historians often write stories with a technical background and cast, books 'whose footnotes have footnotes.' When we are invited onto the public platform, these footnotes have to stay back home. To try to convert three lectures into a technical genre violates both the intentions of the original presentation and the nature of the technical work," he noted. ". . . But the short book based on lectures has its distinct function, and I hope this one fulfills something of it: that is, to start to advance a conversation between town and gown, among academics and citizens at large." In that spirit, I offer these lectures in their published form, with thanks to both Stetson University, which sponsored them, and the University of Georgia Press, which published them.

Although I designed each lecture to stand alone so that my listeners need not attend every one, the lectures as a series develop a common theme in roughly chronological order. The first lecture explores the cultural and scientific response to Darwinism in the United States and Britain, focusing on the late nineteenth century, with some consideration of later developments. The second lecture discusses the American controversy over teaching evolution in public schools, beginning with the antievolution crusade of the 1920s, but again carrying the story forward. In the third lecture I focus on the present, though with some historical context, as I examine the religious views of American scientists. Throughout, we find a rich interplay of science and religion in the tapestry of American culture. In the third lecture, I refer to a series of surveys of American scientists regarding their religious beliefs, including two surveys that I conducted with journalist Larry

Witham during the 1990s. The production of these lectures in book form permits me to add an appendix that reprints the findings of those surveys in a form more complete than previously available. As is common in public lectures, I drew on my previously published work in composing them—and that selective borrowing is apparent in the published version as well.

Through his generous support of these lectures, George H. Shriver continues his legacy of service to the history of religion in America. As a distinguished historian, he helped to build the field. As a donor, his generosity is helping to sustain it. I was particularly pleased that George Shriver attended these lectures, and I benefited from his comments. My thanks go as well to Professor Mitchell Reddish, who organized the events surrounding the lecture, and to Stetson University president Doug Lee and his wife, Margaret, who hosted a dinner at their home. With family in the area, I have watched DeLand change over the years. Stetson now stands at the heart of a vibrant and growing community. With new ties to the university forged by my participation in this lecture series, I look forward to continued interaction with the scholars and students of Stetson in the years ahead.

The Creation-Evolution Debate

DARWINISM AND
THE VICTORIAN SOUL

I have read your book with more pain than pleasure," Cambridge geologist Adam Sedgwick wrote sadly to Charles Darwin within a week of receiving a prepublication copy of his former student's *On the Origin of Species* in 1859. "'Tis the crown & glory of organic science that it *does* thro' *final cause*, link material to moral. . . . You have ignored this link; &, if I do not mistake your meaning, you have done your best in one of two pregnant cases to break it. Were it possible (which thank God it is not) to break it, humanity in my mind, would suffer a damage that might brutalize it."

Writing to Darwin after he received his advance copy of the book, Harvard botanist Asa Gray also expressed concern about its theological implications. "I had no intention to write atheistically," Darwin replied to Gray. "But I own that I cannot see as plainly as others do . . . evidence of design & beneficence on all sides of us. There seems to me too much misery in the world. I cannot persuade myself that a beneficent & omnipotent God would have designedly created the Ichneumonidae with the express intention of their feeding within the living bodies of Caterpillars." Alluding to William Paley's famous analogy between a crafted watch and the human eye, Darwin then noted, "Not believing this, I see no necessity in the belief that the eye was expressedly designed." Even human nature and mental ability might result from natural processes, he added.

The sequence in Darwin's letter to Gray is telling. It passed quickly from observations of what seemed bad in nature (such as cruel animal behavior) to implications for what seemed good in it (such as the human eye), and then moved on to ponder the origin of what seemed best of all, human morality and mentality. In *Origin of Species*, Darwin avoided making comments about human evolution, fearing that they would prejudice readers against his general theory, but his private notes, essays, and letters reveal his long-standing fascination with the issue. Indeed, his earliest private notebooks on evolution are peppered with comparisons between the native peoples of Tierra del Fuego, whom he met during his *Beagle* voyage and considered the lowest form of humanity, and primates in the London zoo.

"Let man visit orangutan in domestication, hear expressive whine, see its intelligence," Darwin wrote in 1838, "then let him dare to boast of his proud preeminence." Here he inserted the phrase, "not understanding language of Fuegian[s], puts [them] on par with Monkeys." In a later entry, Darwin demanded: "Compare, the Fuegian & Orangutan, & dare to say difference so great." He frequently speculated about animal origins of human traits, such as when he wrote, "One's tendency to kiss, & almost to bite, that which one sexually loves is probably . . . due to our distant ancestors have been like *dogs* to bitches." As for the vaunted "mind of man," Darwin concluded, it "is no more perfect, than instincts of animals." Human thought itself (like animal instincts) he attributed to brain structure, chiding himself "oh you Materialist!" for thinking so. Continually he probed questions regarding the perceived boundary between the animal and the human. "Does a negress blush? I am almost sure [the Fuegians] did," he asks himself at one point. "Animals I should think would not."

While Darwin avoided commenting publicly on human evolution, his most visible scientific supporter, naturalist T. H. Huxley, took up the cause and made it his own. In 1863, he packaged the pieces of his various arguments on the topic into a single popular study, *Evidence as to Man's Place in Nature.* "Whatever system of organs be studied," Huxley concluded, "the structural differences that separate Man from the Gorilla and the Chimpanzee are not so great as those which separate the Gorilla from the lower apes."

The most vexing questions raised by Darwinism concerned the origin of human mental and moral attributes, particularly altruistic behavior. Could these distinguishing human characteristics have evolved by a naturalistic process, Victorian evolutionists asked, or did God implant them in an evolved human body? Traditionally, Christian theologians had attributed these attributes to an indwelling soul, the existence of which lifted humans above other animals. Scientists generally segregated humans from other animals on this basis as well, going back to Aristotle's theory of a rational soul found only in humans; proceeding through Cartesian dualism, which split physical matter from the human and divine soul; and continuing with, most recently, George Cuvier's division of humans and primates into separate taxonomic orders. Now Huxley, in *Man's Place in Nature*, lumped humans in the same order with other primates and boldly asked, "Is the philanthropist or the saint to give up his endeavours to lead a noble life, because the simplest study of man's nature reveals, at its foundations, all the selfish passions and fierce appetites of the merest quadruped? Is mother-love vile because a hen shows it, or fidelity base because dogs possess it?" These were the new questions of the Darwinian age.

Descent of Man

After steering clear of the intense public debate over human evolution for over a decade, in 1871 Darwin finally articulated his thinking on the subject in *Descent of Man*. "The sole object of this work," he wrote, "is to consider, firstly, whether man, like every other species, is descended from some pre-existing form; secondly, the manner of his development; and thirdly, the value of the differences between the so-called races of man." In his book, Darwin raised the key issues that would thereafter occupy researchers in the field.

Darwin's basic case for human evolution consisted of two main parts. First, he presented the by-then well-known evidence for the evolution of the human body. In anatomic structure and embryonic development, people resemble other animals, he noted, and the persistence of monkeylike rudimentary features, such as the tailbone, reinforce the conclusion that the human body evolved from lower forms. Relying primarily on structural similarities, Darwin traced human ancestry from "the most ancient progenitors in the kingdom of the Vertebrata," through ancient fishes and amphibians, and early marsupials and placental animals, to "the New World and Old World monkeys; and from the latter, at a remote period, [to] Man, the wonder and glory of the Universe."

The body's evolution, even if accepted, did not settle the matter because many believed that humans stood apart from animals because of their minds and emotions, not their bodies. Darwin thus extended his naturalistic analysis to include those mental and moral attributes that supposedly uplifted humanity, such as higher reasoning, self-consciousness, religious devotion, and the ability to love. The mental powers and moral feelings of humans differed in degree, rather than in kind, from those of other animals, he asserted, with a progressive gradient linking the lowest beasts to the highest humans.

Darwin stressed the humanlike qualities of higher animals, particularly pet dogs and wild monkeys, and the animal-like qualities of the "lowest" savages. "Can we feel sure that an old dog with an excellent memory . . . never reflects on his past pleasures in the chase? and this be a form of self-consciousness," he wrote in a typical passage. "On the other hand, . . . how little can the hard-working wife of a degraded Australian savage . . . reflect on the nature of her own existence!" Similarly, Darwin doubted whether Fuegians felt religious devotion yet saw "some distinct approach to this state of mind in the deep love of a dog for his master."

Darwin attributed the evolution of even the most ennobling of human traits to gradual, survival-of-the-fittest processes. Long ago in Africa, he suggested, some anthropoidal apes descended from the trees, started walking erect in the open spaces, began using their hands to hold or to hunt, and developed their brains—all in incremental steps that helped to preserve the individual or its group. As in *Origin of Species*, the variations themselves were either inborn or acquired, with beneficial ones propagated through natural selection. Darwin envisioned the winnowing process at work among individuals, nationalities, races, and civilizations, with plucky Englishmen (and their American scion) advancing to the fore.

Yet for all the power that Darwin attributed to natural selection in molding humanity and guiding its advance, he saw the process as incapable of generating gender and external racial differences. For those, Darwin resorted to and elaborated on the secondary process of sexual selection that he had introduced in *Origin of Species* to account for the evolution of male mating traits, such as the peacock's tail.

Peoples differ in what they find attractive in mates, Darwin explained. Africans prefer dark skin and depressed noses while Europeans favor light skin and straight noses, he asserted, while "in Java, a yellow, not a white girl, is considered . . . a beauty." Within each race, Darwin speculated, sexual selection propagates and exaggerates favored external characteristics, as the most attractive mates are chosen first and have the most children. For instance, he suggested that Hottentot women have large bottoms because tribesmen desire mates who display that trait. Gender differences arise in a similar fashion, Darwin added, as "the strongest and most vigorous men . . . have been able to select the more attractive women" and together they "would have succeeded in rearing a greater average number of offspring." Thanks to sexual selection, Darwin concluded, men possess greater strength and intellect while women display more beauty and tenderness.

Wallace and Company React

Descent of Man offered the first comprehensive naturalistic theory of human evolution, but it did not change many minds. Europeans and Americans had hotly debated the proposition that humans evolved from beasts since the publication of *Origin of Species* in 1859, but most continued to reject the idea long after the appearance of *Descent of Man* in 1871, including many evolutionists within Darwin's inner circle. For example, the codiscoverer of selection theory, Alfred Russel Wallace, a staunch Darwinist on other matters, became persuaded that an "Overruling Intelligence" created the first humans by ennobling anthropoidal apes with enlightened minds. "Natural selection could only have endowed the savage with a brain a little superior to that of an ape," he wrote in an 1869 article in the *Quarterly Review* and maintained ever after, "whereas he actually possesses one but very little inferior to that of the average members of our learned societies." Darwin's mentor and friend, the geologist Charles Lyell, promptly endorsed Wallace's position, much to Darwin's dismay. For his part, Asa Gray steadfastly maintained that God supervised the beneficial variations that produced humankind.

The triumph of evolutionism within the Victorian scientific community during the 1860s did not translate into widespread popular acceptance of the theory, at least with respect to human origin. Science did not then dominate how Europeans and Americans viewed the natural world—much less the supernatural. The matter of human origin was particularly sensitive because it impacted how people viewed themselves, other persons, and God. Crucially, evolutionary naturalism undermined belief in an indwelling spiritual soul, which for many people defined the very essence of humanness. The doctrine that God specially created the first people by giving them eternal souls held certain implications about the meaning of human life; the theory that humans evolved naturally from soulless animals held others—and many individuals found such a switch difficult. An 1871 cartoon in the British magazine *Punch* captured the tension. It showed an earnest young husband reading to his wife and infant child from Darwin's just-published *Descent of Man*. "So you see, Mary, baby is descended from a hairy quadruped, with pointed ears and a tail. We all are," he explained. His wife countered, "Speak for yourself, Jack. I'm not descended from anything of the kind, I beg to say; and baby takes after me."

The wife's statement articulated the general mood. Late in his life, Wallace could claim, with some hyperbole, that "all of the greatest writers and thinkers" agreed "that the higher mental and spiritual nature of man is not the mere animal nature advanced through survival of the fittest." Novelist Leo Tolstoy proclaimed this viewpoint in Russia, for example, and prominent liberal minister Henry Ward Beecher did so in the United States. Both embraced evolutionism to a point but maintained that only God could make a soul. Roman Catholic Church doctrine fitfully gravitated toward accepting a similar position. During the late 1800s, British prime minister William Gladstone made a point of endorsing the divine creation of humankind.

Whether expressed in scientific commentary or in editorial cartoons, the basic sentiment was similar: Most people simply refused to believe that their highly developed minds, morals, or emotions evolved from those of beasts. The gap appeared to be too great. They felt themselves superior to other animals.

For many, these feelings carried more weight than an abstract scientific theory. "Really, Mr. Darwin," a stylish woman said to a tailed, apish-looking Darwin in an 1872 editorial cartoon response to his *Expression of Emotions in Man and Animals*, which immediately followed *Descent of Man*, "say what you like about man; but I wish you would leave my emotions alone!"

Choosing Sides

Much as some people instinctively rejected the idea of human evolution, others embraced it for reasons that had little to do with science. Before the advent of Darwinism, materialists, atheists, and radical secularists had long displayed fondness for evolutionary theories of origins, such as the one proposed by Lamarck in 1798—anything to dispense with God. Even though Darwin held strictly conventional political and economic views, his theory attracted the usual antiestablishment crowd. Huxley and German biologist Ernst Haeckel initially embraced Darwinism in part because it supported their anticlerical agendas for science and society. In the United States, feminist leader Elizabeth Cady Stanton welcomed Darwinism as a means to undermine what she saw as biblically based arguments for the subordination of women. "The real difficulty in woman's case is that the whole foundation of the Christian religion rests on her temptation and man's fall," she wrote in *The Woman's Bible*. "If, however, we accept the Darwinian theory, that the race has been a gradual growth from the lower to a higher form of life, and the story of the fall is a myth, we can exonerate the snake, emancipate the woman, and reconstruct a more rational religion for the nineteenth century."

From the conservative end of the political spectrum, the enormously influential social philosopher Herbert Spencer, already an evolutionist, freely worked Darwinian materialism into his progressivist philosophy of social development. As social theorists, Spencer and Darwin became inexorably linked in the public mind during the late nineteenth century. Spencer's many followers, whose numbers comprised a virtual social register of the Anglo-American moneyed elite, typically embraced Darwinism as well. In his autobiography, industrialist Andrew Carnegie recalled the day in the 1870s that his reading of Darwin's *Descent of Man* and various books by Spencer transformed his life. "I remember that light came as in a flood and all was clear. Not only had I got rid of theology and the supernatural, but I had found the truth of evolution," he wrote. "Man was not created with an instinct for his own degradation, but from the lower he had risen to the higher forms."

For people like Carnegie, Darwinism became a religion or an alternative to religion. This sentiment appeared pictorially in a popular 1883 poster, attributed to London secularist George Holyoake, which purported to illustrate the fragmentation of the established British "National Church" into various factions ranging from High Church and Roman Catholicism to dissent and rationalism. In the upper left corner, under the banner of "Darwinism," an ape leads Spencer, Huxley, and other "agnostics" away from the central, umbrella-like dome of London's St. Paul's Cathedral toward a distant cloud of "Protoplasm." A bust of Darwin rises above the cloud. With his great white beard, Darwin could as readily appear god-like as he could apish—and during the late nineteenth century, illustrators pictured him both ways. How people viewed Darwin had less to do with science than with society.

In some ways, little has changed in the past century. Many otherwise committed evolutionists draw the line on materialism when it comes to the ascent of man. For example, Oxford ornithologist David Lack, whose landmark 1947 book, *Darwin's Finches*, gave wing to the modern neo-Darwinian interpretation of how evolution is driven by the natural selection of genetic variations, nevertheless said of the higher attributes of humans, "Science has not accounted for morality, truth, beauty, individual responsibility or self-awareness, and many people hold that, from its nature, it can never do so." Similarly, the noted American geneticist Francis Collins, who has directed the human genome project since the 1990s, wrote in a 2002 article titled "Human Genetics," "Science will certainly not shed any light on what it means to love someone, what it means to have a spiritual dimension to our existence, nor will it tell us much about the character of God." Opinion surveys suggest that Collins speaks for about 40 percent of the American people and up to a like percentage of American scientists when he posits God as somehow involved in the evolutionary process, at least to the extent of breathing a supernaturally created soul into a naturally evolved body. For the record, the Roman Catholic Church approves the latter position. "Rather than *the* theory of evolution, we should speak of *several* theories of evolution . . . materialistic, reductionist and spiritualist," Pope John Paul II declared in a 1996 message to the Pontifical Academy of Sciences. "Theories of evolution which, in accordance with the philosophies inspiring them, consider the mind as emerging from the forces of living matter, or as a mere epiphenomenon of this matter, are incompatible with the truth about man."

From the very outset, it was this prospect that humans evolved from primates that people found most intriguing in Darwinism. Although Sedgwick closed his 1859 letter to Darwin with a lighthearted reference to himself as "a son of a monkey," he never gave ground on a divine source for the human soul. For him and most other Victorians, as for many today, that was no laughing matter.

THE AMERICAN CONTROVERSY
OVER CREATION AND EVOLUTION

The American controversy over creation and evolution is primarily fought over what is taught in U.S. public high school biology classes. Virtually no one disputes teaching the theory of evolution in public colleges and universities or using public funding to support evolutionary research in agriculture or medicine. And there is no serious debate over the core evolutionary concept of common descent among biologists. It is the minds of American high school students that are at stake, and opponents of evolutionary teaching typically ask for (1) removing evolutionary biology from the classroom, or (2) balancing it with some form of creationist instruction, or (3) teaching it in some fashion as "just a theory." Actually these three strategies, although always present to some extent, also play out chronologically as to when they have dominated so as to create three discernable phases of antievolutionism, with the first two serving as a prologue to the current third.

Phase 1: The Antievolution Crusade

The 1925 trial of John Scopes highlights the phase of anti-evolutionism characterized by efforts to remove the theory of evolution from the high school biology classroom altogether. Importantly, this effort coincided with and arose out of the so-called Fundamentalist crisis with American Protestantism, when many mainline Protestant denominations—the Presbyterians, Methodists, American Baptists, and others—were deeply divided between the so-called modernists, who adapted their traditional beliefs to current scientific thinking, and a new breed of Fundamentalists who clung even tighter to biblical literalism in the face of new ideas.

No idea split the modernists from the Fundamentalists more than the Darwinian theory of human evolution—and the rift was aggravated by the seeming rise in agnosticism among the cultural and scientific elite. From the first, the Fundamentalist-modernist controversy raged over the interpretation of Genesis at the pulpit. By the twenties, both sides had carried that theological dispute into the classroom. Neither side wanted the other's view taught as fact in public-school biology courses. In 1922, Fundamentalists across the land began lobbying for laws against teaching the Darwinian theory of human evolution in public schools, leading to the passage of the first such statute in Tennessee during the spring of 1925. Lesser restrictions had already been imposed in other places, and like the current debate over intelligent design, the issue had gained national attention.

From the outset, the so-called antievolution crusade was seen as evidence of a new and profound cleavage between traditional values and modernity. I use the term "evidence" advisedly. The antievolution crusade did not cause the cleavage—it simply exposed it. Go back a generation or two before the twenties, and Americans tended to share common values (or at least those Americans of Protestant European roots that set the tone). Mid-nineteenth-century America had atheists, agnostics, and deists, but they were marginal, and theological disputes among Christians rarely disrupted denominational harmony. Even the academy was a conventionally religious place—that is, until the rise, late in the nineteenth century, of empirical, naturalistic, and historicist modes of discourse and investigation like positivism, biblical higher criticism, and Darwinism. By the early twentieth century, surveys and studies began detecting a widening gap between the God-fearing American majority and the disbelieving cultural elite. It was not that the elite wanted to reject God and biblical revelation, commentator Walter Lippmann explained at the time, but rather that the ascendancy of rational, naturalistic modes of analysis made them unbelievable. Indeed, the heart of modernity lay in the scientific method being applied to all facets of life more than in any particular scientific theory—but

Darwinism was critical in applying that method to the key issues of biological origins and human morality.

The Tennessee antievolution statute thus struck a chord that resonated widely. The nationwide attention garnered by its passage soon focused on Dayton when a local science teacher named John Scopes accepted the invitation of the ACLU to challenge it in court. The media promptly proclaimed the case "the trial of the century," as this young teacher (backed by the nation's scientific, educational, and cultural establishment) stood against the forces of Fundamentalist religious lawmaking. For many Americans at the time and ever after, the *Scopes* trial represented the inevitable conflict between newfangled scientific thought and old-fashioned supernatural belief.

Like so many archetypal American events, the trial itself began as a publicity stunt. Inspired by the ACLU's offer to defend any Tennessee schoolteacher willing to defy the new antievolution statute, Dayton civic leaders saw a chance to gain attention for their struggling young community by hosting a test case of the law. "The town boomers leaped to accept as one man," the journalist H. L. Mencken noted at the time. "Here was an unexampled, almost a miraculous chance to get Dayton upon the front pages, to make it talked about, to put it upon the map." Scopes became the willing defendant at the invitation of school officials. The young teacher was neither jailed nor ostracized and spent much of the time until his trial traveling and talking with reporters. Of course, the ill-conceived scheme quickly backfired on Dayton when the national media indicted the town for indicting one if its teachers—the story was simply too good to pass up. The real story, however, was that Tennessee had passed its antievolution statute in the first place, and that story had long roots.

Ever since Charles Darwin published his theory of evolution in 1859, some conservative Christians objected to the atheistic implications of its naturalistic explanation for the origins of species, particularly of humans. Further, some traditional scientists—most notably the great Harvard zoologist Louis Agassiz—promptly challenged the very notion of biological evolution by arguing that highly complex individual organs, such as the eye, and ecologically dependent species, such as bees and flowers, could not evolve through the sort of minute, random steps envisioned by Darwinism. Although the scientific community largely converted to the new theory due to its ability to explain other natural phenomena that appear utterly senseless under a theory of design or creation, such as the fossil record and the geographic distribution of similar species, religious opposition remained, with these religious opponents often invoking earlier scientific arguments against evolution. These religious objections naturally intensified with the spread of Fundamentalism during the early twentieth century.

The legendary American politician and orator William Jennings Bryan, a political progressive with decidedly orthodox religious beliefs, added his voice to this chorus during the twenties, as he came to see Darwinian survival-of-the-fittest thinking, known as Social Darwinism when applied to human society, as being behind World War I militarism and postwar materialism. Of course, Bryan also had religious objections to Darwinism, and he invoked Agassiz's scientific arguments against it as well — but his fervor on this issue arose from his social concerns. Equate humans with other animals as the product of purely natural processes, Bryan reasoned, and they will act like apes. With his progressive political instinct of seeking legislative solutions to social problems, Bryan campaigned for laws against teaching the Darwinian theory of human evolution in public schools, leading directly to the passage of Tennessee's antievolution statute in 1925. He then volunteered to assist the prosecution when his law was challenged in Dayton, foreseeing the pending show trial as a platform from which to promote his cause.

The prospect of Bryan using the trial to defend biblical religion and attack Darwinism drew Clarence Darrow. By the twenties, Darrow unquestionably stood out as the most famous criminal-defense attorney in the United States. Darrow's trials were sensational, as he pioneered new techniques for the selection of juries, the cross-examination, and the closing argument to defend his typically notorious clients in bitterly hostile courts. Outside the courtroom, Darrow used his celebrity status and oratorical skills to challenge traditional morality and religion. At the time, most Americans clung to biblical notions of right and wrong, and Darrow's defendants were usually quite wrong. Darrow, however, with his modern mind, saw nothing as really wrong (or right)—morality and ethics were culturally or biologically determined. For him, dogmatic beliefs springing from revealed religion were usually the real culprit because they imposed narrow standards of behavior, divided Americans into sects, and made people judgmental. While Bryan hailed God as love and Christ as the Prince of Peace, Darrow damned religion as hateful and Christianity as the cause of war. Indeed, Darrow saw rational science—particularly the theory of organic evolution—as offering a more humane perspective than any irrational religion. Such opinions left no grounds for compromise between the two men on this issue. Both men were affable enough—and they actually cooperated on some issues—but their worldviews were at war.

The drama of Bryan and Darrow litigating the issues of revealed religion versus naturalistic science and academic freedom versus popular control over public education turned the trial into a media sensation then and the stuff of legend thereafter. The trial attracted hundreds of reporters to Dayton and generated front-page stories around the world. Broadcast live over the radio, in time, it became the subject of Broadway plays, Hollywood movies, and Nashville songs. Clearly *Scopes* remains the best-known misdemeanor trial in American history. Despite Darrow's eloquent pleas for academic freedom and his humiliating cross-examination of Bryan, Scopes ultimately lost the case, and Tennessee's antievolution statute was upheld. In large part, this resulted from the fact that the U.S. Supreme Court had not yet extended the constitutional bar against government establishment of religion to public schools.

When the trial was finished, most neutral observers viewed it as a draw so far as public opinion was concerned. The adversarial legal system of the United States tends to drive parties apart rather than reconcile them. That was certainly the result in this case. Despite Bryan's stumbling on the witness stand, which his supporters attributed to his notorious interrogator's wiles, both sides effectively communicated their message from Dayton—maybe not well enough to win converts but at least sufficiently enough to energize those already predisposed toward a particular viewpoint. If, as the defense claimed, more Americans became alert to the danger of placing limits on teaching evolution, others—particularly Evangelical Christians—became even more concerned about the spiritual and social implications of Darwinian instruction.

Consequently, the pace of antievolution activism actually quickened after the trial, especially in the South, but it encountered aroused popular resistance everywhere. Arkansas and Mississippi soon followed Tennessee in outlawing the teaching of human evolution, for example, but when one Rhode Island legislator introduced such a proposal in 1927, his bemused colleagues referred it to the Committee on Fish and Game, where it died without a hearing or a vote. A forty-year standoff resulted in which a hodgepodge of state and local

limits on teaching evolution coupled with heightened paren-
tal concern elsewhere led most high school biology textbooks
and many individual teachers virtually to ignore the subject
of organic origins voluntarily. As a result, after the Tennessee
Supreme Court reversed Scopes's conviction on a technicality,
courts did not have another chance to review antievolution
laws until the 1960s. By then, the legal landscape had changed
dramatically.

Phase 2: The Creation-Science Movement

The change began in 1947, when the U.S. Supreme Court
grafted the First Amendment bar against government establishment of religion to the individual liberties protected
from state action by the Fourteenth Amendment. Suddenly
the establishment clause took on new life. Whereas Congress
had rarely made laws respecting the establishment of religion
prior to 1947 — so there was little case law on point — states
and their public schools had been doing so right along. Hence,
a torrent of establishment clause litigation resulted. Soon
Scopes-like legal battles over the place of religion in public
education erupted in communities across the land, giving the
old trial new relevance everywhere.

The first of these cases did not address restrictions on
teaching evolution, but they surely implicated them. In suc-
cessive decisions beginning in 1948, the U.S. Supreme Court
struck down classroom religious instruction, school-sponsored
prayer, mandatory bible reading, and, in 1968, antievolution

laws. These old laws simply banned the teaching of human evolution—they did not authorize teaching other theories. Indeed, in his day, Bryan never called for including any form of creationist instruction in the science classroom because no scientific alternative to evolution then existed. Even he believed that the biblical days of creation symbolized vast ages of geologic time and said as much on the witness stand in Dayton. But with the publication of *The Genesis Flood* in 1961, Virginia Tech engineering professor Henry Morris gave believers scientific-sounding arguments supporting the biblical account of a six-day creation within the past ten thousand years. This book spawned a movement within American Fundamentalism, with Morris as its Moses leading the faithful into a promised land where science proved religion. The appearance of so-called creation science, or scientific creationism (its proponents use both terms), launched the second phase of antievolution politics: seeking balanced treatment for creation as a theory alongside evolution.

Creation science spread within the conservative Protestant church through the missionary work of Morris's Institute for Creation Research. The emergence of the Religious Right carried it into politics during the 1970s. Within two decades after the publication of *The Genesis Flood,* three states and dozens of local school districts had mandated "balanced treatment" for creation science alongside evolution in public-school science courses. Another decade would pass before the U.S. Supreme Court would unravel those balanced-treatment mandates as unconstitutional. Creation science was nothing but religion dressed up as science, the High Court decreed in the 1987 decision *Edwards v. Aguillard*, in which Justice Antonin Scalia dissented, and therefore was barred by the establishment clause from public-school classrooms along with other forms of religious instruction. By this time, however, conservative Christians were entrenched in local and state politics from California to Maine and deeply concerned about science education.

Phase 3: Intelligent Design

Along came University of California law professor Phillip Johnson and the third phase of the creation-evolution controversy. Johnson is—or, at least then, was—no young-earth creationist, but he is an Evangelical Protestant with an uncompromising faith in God. His target became both the philosophical belief and methodological practice within science that material entities subject to physical laws account for everything in nature. Whether called "naturalism" or "materialism," such a philosophy or method excludes God from science laboratories and classrooms. "The important thing is not whether God created all at once [as scientific creationism holds] or in stages [as progressive creationism or theistic evolution maintain]," Johnson asserted in a 1997 *Christianity Today* interview. "Anyone who thinks that the biological world is a product of a pre-existing intelligence . . . is a creationist in the most important sense of the word. By this broad definition at least eighty percent of Americans, including me, are creationists." Darwinism may be the best naturalistic explanation for the origin of species, he stresses in his writing, but it could still be wrong. If public schools cannot teach creation science because it promotes the tenants of a particular religion, then scientific evidence of design in nature or at least scientific dissent from evolution theory should be permissible, Johnson argues. After all, evolution is "just a theory," he says, and not a very good one.

Johnson's books have sold nearly a half million copies, so it is no wonder that his kind of arguments now show up whenever objections are raised against teaching evolution in public schools. His ideas were apparent in the U.S. Senate in 2001 when Pennsylvania senator Rick Santorum offered legislation encouraging teachers "to make distinctions between philosophical materialism and authentic science and to include unanswered questions and unsolved problems in their presentations of the origins of life and living things." That language, penned by Johnson, passed the Senate as an amendment to the No Child Left Behind education bill and eventually became part of the conference report for that legislation. Similar proposals have surfaced as stand-alone bills in over a dozen state legislatures during the past four years. Though none of the bills have passed, the language has made its way into state and local school guidelines around the country, most famously in Kansas state and in Dover, Pennsylvania.

Another popular authority on this topic is Lehigh University biochemistry professor Michael Behe, a devout Catholic who wrote his own best-selling book challenging Darwinist explanations for complex biological processes and, most recently, who served as the star witness for the defense in the challenge to the Dover school guidelines. If Johnson is the modern movement's Bryan, Behe is its Agassiz reviving the arguments for design based on evidence of nature's irreducible complexity. For Agassiz, those arguments relied on complexity at the organismic and organic levels; for Behe, it's all in the cells. Behe has never developed his arguments for the intelligent design of cellular processes in peer-reviewed science articles. Indeed, he does not actually conduct research in the field and, along with other leaders of the Intelligent Design movement, concedes that there is not as yet much affirmative scientific content to their so-called design revolution. "You'll get a lot of scientists who will stand up and say, 'Sure we don't know how the complexity of the cell evolved,'" Behe acknowledged in a 2006 interview on National Public Radio. "But if you want to get somebody [in science] to stand up and say, 'I think the complexity of the cell points to design,' then the numbers go down to me and a couple others." Ultimately, there is no science of Intelligent Design because the underlying concept raises philosophical rather than scientific questions that cannot be studied using the scientific method, at least as that method is defined and applied. Reflecting this, although the preface to the 1998 book *Mere Creation*, which featured contributions from Behe and other leading ID theorists, contained the prediction that a National Science Foundation–funded design-based research program could be up and running within five years, no such program has come into being despite a potentially friendly presidential administration and Congress in Washington.

So far, ID theorists remain simply critics of the reigning paradigm in biology—doggedly poking holes and looking for gaps in evolution theory. Those gaps are best filled by design, they argue, and would be if science did not rule supernatural explanations out of bounds a priori. ID advocates now propose broadening the definition of science from dealing solely with naturalistic explanations for physical phenomena to including any account that draws on physical, observable data and logical inferences. At least, they add, design-based criticism of evolution, divorced from biblical creationism, should be a fit subject for public-school science education. With this approach, they have expanded the tent of people willing to challenge the alleged Darwinist hegemony in the science classroom beyond those persuaded by Morris's evidence for a young earth.

Yet every public-opinion survey suggests that the bedrock for antievolutionism in the United States remains the biblical literalism of the Protestant Fundamentalist church, which typically voices greater concern about the earth's age, to which the Bible speaks, than about such intellectual abstractions as scientific naturalism. In *The Genesis Flood*, for example, Henry Morris stresses the theological significance of utter fidelity to the entire biblical narrative. Thus, when

Genesis says that God created the universe in six days, he maintains, it must mean six twenty-four-hour days; when it says that God created humans and all animals on the sixth day, then dinosaurs must have lived alongside early man; and when it gives a genealogy of Noah's descendants, believers can use it to date the flood at between five thousand and seven thousand years ago.

Creation versus Evolution in the Twenty-first Century

Despite judicial rulings against the incorporation of scientific creationism into the public-school biology curriculum, public-opinion surveys suggest that approximately four out of ten Americans accept biblical creationism of the sort espoused by Morris and his Institute for Creation Research. If not propagated in the public schools, then creationism must spread by other means — and conservative Christian religious organizations have the necessary structures in place. Nearly fifty years after its initial publication, *The Genesis Flood*, currently in its forty-second printing, continues to sell well in Christian bookstores but is now only one on a shelf full of such books. Christian radio and television blanket the nation with creationist broadcasts and cablecasts such as Ken Ham's *Answers in Genesis*, which is heard daily on over 750 radio stations in forty-nine states and fifteen countries. Although still relatively low in absolute terms, the number of students receiving their primary and secondary education at home or in Christian academies has steadily risen over the past quarter century, with many such students learning their biology from creationist textbooks. At the postsecondary level, Bible institutes and Christian colleges continue to grow in number and size, with at least some of them offering degrees in biology and science education in a creation-friendly environment.

All this creationist activity is nearly invisible outside the churches and religious communities where it occurs, but that has not stopped some evolutionists from striking back. To be sure, most biologists simply ignore religion. But some of them — ardent in their evolutionism and evangelical regarding its social implications — have taken a Darrowesque dislike to biblical Christianity. The British sociobiologist and popular science writer Richard Dawkins leads this particular pack.

In *The Blind Watchmaker*, published to great acclaim in the midst of legal wrangling over Louisiana's creation-science law, Dawkins takes aim at what he calls "redneck" creationists and "their disturbingly successful fight to subvert American education and textbook publishing." Focusing on the philosophical heart of creationism rather than simple biblical literalism, Dawkins challenges the very notion of purposeful design in nature, which he calls "the most influential of the arguments for the existence of God." In a legendary articulation of the purposeful-design argument in 1802, British theologian William Paley compared living things to mechanical watches. Just as the intricate workings of a watch betray its maker's purposes, Paley reasoned, so too does the even more intricate complexity of an organism and even an individual organ, such as the eye, prove the existence of a purposeful creator. Not so, Dawkins counters. "Natural selection, the blind, unconscious, automatic process which Darwin described, and which we now know is the explanation for the existence and apparently purposeful form of all life, has no purpose. . . . It is the *blind* watchmaker." By banishing the argument for design, Dawkins proclaims, "Darwin made it possible to be an intellectually fulfilled atheist." Renowned Harvard naturalist and science writer E. O. Wilson makes similar assertions. "The inexorable growth of [biology] continues to widen, not to close, the tectonic gap between science and faith-based religion," Wilson wrote in this 2006 book, *From So Simple a Beginning: The Four Great Books of Charles Darwin.* "The toxic mix of religion and tribalism has become so dangerous as to justify taking seriously the alternative view, that humanism based on science is the effective antidote, the light and the way at last placed before us."

Organized science has sought to defuse this controversy by affirming the compatibility of modern evolutionary naturalism with a personal belief in God. The National Academy of Sciences, a self-selecting body of the nation's premiere scientists, asserted as much in a glossy brochure distributed to schoolteachers during the 1980s in reaction to the creation-science movement. In 1998, the academy mass-produced a new booklet reasserting that, although science is committed to methodological naturalism, it does not conflict with religion. Science and religion simply represent separate ways of knowing. "Science," the booklet states, "is limited to explaining the natural world through natural causes. Science can say nothing about the supernatural. Whether God exists or not is a question about which science is neutral." To Dawkins, such an approach represents "a cowardly flabbiness of the intellect." Johnson dismisses it as rank hypocrisy. If they agree on nothing else, Dawkins and Johnson agree that Darwinism and Christianity are at war, and with their writings and talks, they help to stir popular passions over biology education much as Darrow and Bryan once did. We see its fruit even now in pending lawsuits and legislation.

Five years ago in Kansas, for example, creationists on the state school board succeeded temporarily in deleting the big bang and what they called "macroevolution" from the list of topics mandated for coverage in public-school science classrooms. Last year, they took the further step of adding an ID-friendly definition of science to their educational standards. According to those revised standards, "Science is a systematic method of continuing investigation that uses observations, hypothesis testing, measurement, experimentation, logical argument and theory building to lead to more adequate explanations of natural phenomena." Nothing here now rules out the supernatural for explaining the natural. In 2004, the Cobb County, Georgia, school board decreed that biology textbooks should carry a disclaimer stating that evolution was just a theory. Last year, the Dover, Pennsylvania, school board not only mandated an oral disclaimer akin to Cobb County's written one but also recommended Intelligent Design as an alternative explanation of biological origins. In cases that made front-page news across the country and overseas, federal district courts struck down the Cobb County and Dover restrictions. Although one remains under appeal, both rulings are instructive.

Responding to the concerns of local parents and taxpayers, the Cobb County school board had mandated that biology textbooks carry a sticker stating, "Evolution is a theory, not a fact, regarding the origin of living things. This material should be approached with an open mind, studied carefully, and critically considered." Similar disclaimers have appeared in Alabama textbooks for years without sparking lawsuits and are under consideration elsewhere, but, perhaps because of the diverse nature of the county's population and its visible location as a bedroom community for Atlanta, the disclaimer immediately encountered stiff opposition in Cobb County. The Georgia ACLU promptly filed suit on behalf of some local students and their parents.

In his judicial opinion, Judge Clarence Cooper tackled anti-evolutionists' "only a theory" argument. Of course evolution is only a theory, but it's not a hunch or a guess, he noted, adding, "The Sticker targets only evolution to be approached with an open mind, carefully studied, and critically considered without explaining why it is the only theory being so isolated as such." In light of the historic opposition to the theory of evolution by certain religious groups, Judge Cooper concluded that "an informed, reasonable observer would perceive the school board to be aligning itself with proponents of religious theories of origins." As such, the sticker constituted an impermissible endorsement of religion under prevailing constitutional standards, the judge ruled.

Although Judge Cooper did not expand on the point, he identified the group benefited by the sticker as "Christian fundamentalists and creationists," not theists generally. Many people see the controversy this way, which helps to explain its depth. Millions of American Christians and other religious believers accept the theory of evolution. For some theologically liberal Christians, evolution is central to their religious worldview. Even many theologically conservative Protestants and Catholics accept organic evolution as God's means of creation. They see no conflict between it and a high view of scripture. Theistic theories of evolution have a long and distinguished pedigree within Evangelical Christian theology. By cautioning students against all theories of evolution, some saw the Cobb County school board lining up on one side of a dispute among religious believers and in doing so unconstitutionally entangling church and state. Judge Cooper agreed and held this as a second legal basis for striking the stickers.

The Dover case, like the Cobb County one, involved school guidelines built on the ID argument that students should be told that evolution is a controversial and unproven theory. "The theory is not a fact," the Dover disclaimer stated.

"Gaps in the theory exist for which there is not evidence." This alone conveyed an unconstitutional endorsement of a religious viewpoint, the court ruled. Unlike the Cobb County sticker, however, the statement read to Dover students added, "Intelligent Design is an explanation of the origin of life that differs from Darwin's view. The reference book, *Of Pandas and People*, is available for students who might be interested in gaining an understanding of what Intelligent Design actually involves." This text, the court found, contained creationist religious material, including the affirmation that basic kinds of living things, such as birds and fish, were separately created. As such, its use in public education violated the constitutional bar against religious instruction.

The decision went further, though. During a six-week trial, Judge John Jones heard extensive testimony on Intelligent Design to determine whether it could be presented as an alternative explanation of origins in a public-school science class. Here his decision broke new ground. "After a searching review of the record and applicable case law," Judge Jones ruled, "we find that while ID arguments may be true, a proposition on which the Court takes no position, ID is not science." He gave three reasons. First, unlike science, ID invokes supernatural explanations. Second, it rests on the flawed argument that evidence against the current theory of evolution supports the design alternative. Third, scientists have largely refuted the attacks on evolution leveled by ID theorists. ID, the judge stressed, has not been accepted by the scientific community, generated peer-review publications, nor been subjected to testing and research—all points that Michael Behe conceded under cross-examination. Indeed, after offering an alternative definition for science that ID could meet—a proposed explanation that focuses on or points to physical, observable data and logical inferences—Behe admitted that astrology would also qualify as science. This alone probably sealed the decision, but evidence that school board members acted with a clear religious purpose and then tried to cover their tracks also turned this judge, a no-nonsense conservative appointed by President George W. Bush, against the school policy. "The breathtaking inanity of the Board's decision is evident when considered against the factual backdrop which has now been fully revealed through this trial," Judge Jones concluded.

In Dover, as in Cobb County, the school board's decision to adopt the antievolution disclaimer polarized the community. It divided families, neighbors, and churches. In an election held before the court ruled, voters replaced eight members of the school board with candidates opposed to the policy, guaranteeing that it will not appeal the court's ruling. When Americans on either side of this controversy watch what happened in Cobb County or Dover, they know that they are looking in a mirror and wonder how such a case might play out in their own hometown and among their friends and fellow Christians. Of course, the media took notice, making these cases top stories.

That, in brief, is where the creation-evolution teaching

controversy stands today—still making news eighty years after Dayton, Tennessee, gained headlines by prosecuting John Scopes. It resurfaces periodically in countless Daytons throughout the United States over everyday episodes of science teachers either defying or deifying Darwin. Such acts generate lawsuits and legislation precisely because religion continues to matter greatly in America. Public-opinion surveys invariably find that over nine in ten Americans believe in God, just as they have found since polling on such matters began in the 1950s. A recent survey indicated that over three-fourths of Americans believe in miracles and that three out of five find religion "very important" in their lives. It troubles many Americans that science does not affirm their faith and outrages some when their children's biology coursework seems to deny their biblical beliefs.

As a diverse people, Americans have learned to seek middle ground whenever possible. As a species, however, humans instinctively respond to stirring oratory. Darrow and Bryan had mastered that craft and used it in Dayton to enlist their legions. They tapped into a cultural divide that deeply troubled—and continues to trouble—the national house, offering no middle ground. And as we all know, either from the Bible or from a Broadway classic, "He that troubleth his own house shall inherit the wind." That wind has sporadically touched off maelstroms over the past eighty years, storms that sorely test America's tradition of tolerance. If history is any guide, dark clouds remain on the horizon.

SCIENTISTS AND RELIGION
IN AMERICA

The United States increasingly relies on science and the systemic exploitation of the natural world by scientific researchers to fuel its economy, defend its borders, and enhance the health of its people. At the same time, however, the United States remains a deeply religious country where more people than ever appear to be seeking answers to fundamental questions in the supernatural. In a growing body of research, historians, social scientists, and other commentators are exploring how these parallel developments have played out and will continue to play out in practice. Scientists and their beliefs about religion represent a key element in this equation.

Historians of science typically use one or more of three models to explain the relationship between science and religion. Some see conflict, or even warfare, inevitably resulting from the clash between the claims of science and the dogma of religion. The seventeenth-century trial and conviction of Galileo Galilei by the Roman Catholic Church inevitably looms large for these "conflict" historians. Others interpret the interaction of these two ways of knowing as complementary. Johannes Kepler's discovery of the three laws of planetary motion, inspired by his view of God as a geometric designer of the universe, offers a prime example of such a fruitful interplay of ideas. Another group of historians posit that science and religion coexist in separate spheres. For these historians, Gregor Mendel's groundbreaking research on the heredity of pea plants conducted during his devout service as an Austrian monk exemplifies such benign coexistence. These are idealized models, of course, and even the cited examples, if closely examined, do not neatly fit them. Historical evidence usually suggests a much richer complexity at play than any one model can supply. Yet the models do guide historical understanding.

Among Americans, the so-called conflict or warfare model is perhaps the most common way to view the interaction between science and religion, and it also provides the basis for how American scientists often see the relationship. Of course, I'm not talking about an actual war between science and religion, as if mental constructs can fight like countries do, marshalling armies and taking territory. Rather, the model represents how people perceive the relationship between science and religion or, perhaps, what occurs in an individual's mind when confronted with the claims of either one. Although warfare is just a metaphor, the fact that such a metaphor is both seductive and tenacious suggests that people respond to it and feel it has validity.

Metaphors are thrown around all the time, but they only survive if they resonate with people. For example, an American sports promoter once referred to the NCAA basketball tournament as "March Madness," and the metaphor stuck. The tournament does not actually drive basketball fans "mad" in the clinical sense of that term, but the metaphor seemed apt to those who follow the sport. Once the phrase took hold, it helped to feed the "madness." Similarly, some nineteenth-century partisans spoke of "warfare" or "conflict" between science and religion, and that characterization seemed apt enough to people that they used it, which in turn probably reinforced the sense of discord going forward. The warfare metaphor remains as alive today as it was in the past. A brief comparison of the vitality of the metaphor in the nineteenth and twentieth centuries illustrates this point.

The Nineteenth Century

Participants in the science and religion debate have used the Galileo affair to bolster their arguments for over three centuries. In the seventeenth century, Protestants used it to club Catholicism. During the eighteenth century, Enlightenment secularists turned it on all of Christianity. And in the nineteenth century, secularists applied it against religion in general. As evidence, American historians widely cite two histories of the "conflict" published in the United States during the nineteenth century, one by John William Draper and the other by Andrew Dickson White. Neither Draper nor White were primarily historians, however. Draper was a chemist, and White had become a college president. Many other nineteenth-century histories, by contrast, presented religion as fostering science, with some Protestant historians claiming that the Reformation jump-started science, and some Catholic historians praising the Roman Church's support for science. Thus, as history, the works of Draper and White were not necessarily representative of their time. Further, they did not so much attack religion generally as Catholicism in particular. This was especially true of Draper's book. The view that science was at war with all religion did not dominate nineteenth-century American historical thought.

Further, the various nineteenth-century interpretations of the relationship between science and religion — from warfare to collaboration — did not solely appear in works of history. Scientists also expressed these views, with a diversity similar to those expressed by historians. During the nineteenth century, the warfare thesis appears in the writings of such prominent British scientists as Charles Lyell, Charles Darwin, T. H. Huxley, and Francis Galton, all of whom were extraordinarily influential in the United States. These scholars typically focused their fury on Catholicism, but other religions could suffer their assaults as well. Huxley made this explicit in his published essay collection *Science and Christian Tradition*.

"From the earliest times of which we have any knowledge, Naturalism [or science] and Supernaturalism [or religion] have consciously, or unconsciously, competed and struggled with one another," he wrote. Protestants joined with secularists in using science to debunk Catholicism, Huxley noted, but "their alliance was bound to be of short duration, and, sooner or later, to be replaced by internecine warfare." Here is the warfare thesis expressed by a combatant in the fray—and so it should carry considerable evidentiary weight.

At the same time, however, other scientists were expressing very different views of the relationship between science and religion—Lord Kelvin, James Clerk Maxwell, or Michael Faraday, for instance. These British physicists carried similar stature as Lyell, Darwin, and Huxley in the United States and Europe, yet none of them declared war on religion. Quite to the contrary, they saw science and religion as complementary. In the United States, the eminent nineteenth-century botanist Asa Gray lectured on the compatibility of Darwinian biology and biblical Christianity. In short, although the warfare thesis was alive and well in nineteenth-century thought, it did not go unchallenged. Historians did not uniformly preach it, and scientists did not uniformly confess it.

Twentieth Century and Beyond

A similar diversity of opinion on the relationship between science and religion existed during the twentieth century and continues into the twenty-first. At least in the United States, the period has witnessed a continuing divide between science and religion, with both flourishing in their separate spheres. Housed in ever-expanding research universities and fueled by unprecedented amounts of public funding, American science has assumed global leadership in virtually every scientific discipline. The technological payoff has transformed American industry, agriculture, and warfare. At the same time, surveys have found that a greater percentage of Americans regularly attend religious services and profess belief in God than the people of any other scientifically advanced nation—with no apparent decline over time. Yet surveys also suggest that these percentages drop off precipitously for American scientists, particularly at the higher echelons of the profession. This provides a context in which some conservative Christians can denounce objectionable scientific theories as the work of "atheists."

Perhaps the most significant development in the relationship between science and American religion over the past two centuries within the religious community has been the disengagement of mainline Protestantism from the science and religion dialogue. In the wake of William Paley's popular works of natural theology, mainline Anglo-American Protestants regularly invoked science in support of their religious beliefs during the nineteenth century and sought to reconcile science with religion. In marked contrast, such preeminent twentieth-century Protestant theologians as Karl Barth, Paul Tillich, and Reinhold Niebuhr virtually ignored science in their theological writings. Mainline Protestants joined most Catholics in largely reserving their comments about science to ethical issues raised by new technologies, such as biotechnology or nuclear weapons, and to making the general observation that modern theories such as the big bang and quantum indeterminacy leave room for God.

During the twentieth century, however, Evangelical, Fundamentalist, and Pentecostal churches have displaced mainline ones as the center of gravity within American Protestantism. Many in these churches feel that their beliefs are under siege from science — particularly from Darwinism but also from dominant theories in geology, cosmology, and psychology — and some of them militantly lash out against these threatening ideas. In this context, lay Christians periodically have stirred mass movements against the theory of organic evolution over the past century, as was discussed in detail in the previous chapter. Presbyterian politician William Jennings Bryan did so in the 1920s, resulting in legal limits on the teaching of evolution in some public schools and the 1925 trial of high school teacher John Scopes for violating one such law in Tennessee. Beginning in the 1960s, Baptist engineering professor Henry Morris helped to revive a literal reading of the Genesis account of creation among conservative Protestants, prompting widespread demands for teaching so-called creation science alongside Darwinism in biology classes. And in the 1990s, Presbyterian law professor Phillip Johnson rekindled interest among conservative Christians for

pre-Darwinian concepts of intelligent design in nature, leading to demands that public schools modify the science curriculum to incorporate their concerns.

Each of these episodes have breathed new life into the warfare thesis and evoked comparisons to Galileo's persecution.
Scopes's defenders frequently compared the young Tennessee
schoolteacher to Galileo, for example, with his defense counsel
at one point in the trial declaring, "Every scientific discovery
or new invention has been met by the opposition of people
like those behind this prosecution who have pretended that
man's inventive genius was contrary to Christianity." The
lead prosecutor responded, "They say it is a battle between
religion and science, and in the name of God, I stand with
religion." Similarly, both Morris and Johnson have presented
Darwinian science as at war with Christianity, and some scientists have responded in kind. As noted in the previous chapter, for example, British biologist Richard Dawkins takes aim
at religious creationists in his book *The Blind Watchmaker*.
And in his 2006 book, *From So Simple a Beginning*, the extraordinary influential American biologist E. O. Wilson asks,
"So, will science and religion find common ground, or at least
agree to divide the fundamentals into mutually exclusive do-
main?" In giving his answer to this question, he rejects both
of these approaches, which reflect the complimentary and coexistence models for science and religion. "The battle line is,
as it has ever been, biology," Wilson writes.

The warfare model survives among American historians as

well. To be sure, some prominent historians have begun reassessing the historical relations between science and religion, shifting from "cold war" to "frank dialogue." But other historians still speak in terms of a conflict between the two ways of thinking. Taking their cue from Morris and Johnson, for example, religious opponents of Darwinian naturalism interpret modern history in terms of a clash between Christian values and evolutionary ethics. Much of this work is by nonhistorians — such as Morris and Johnson themselves, who blame all manner of modern "evil," including communism and total war, on Darwinism — but followers of the Morris and Johnson tradition also include trained historians, such as California State University history professor Richard Weikart, whose 2002 book, *From Darwin to Hitler*, roots Nazi barbarism in scientific naturalism and in Hitler's repudiation of traditional Christian values. On the other side, even such mainstream history-of-science texts as *Science and Technology in World History*, by James McClellan and Harold Dorn, which I use in some of my introductory courses, perpetuate the warfare thesis, beginning with the comment that Thales, the first Greek natural philosopher, "sets the natural world off somehow separate from the divine" and continuing through vivid depictions of the Galileo affair and modern Christian opposition to Darwinism. For McClellan and Dorn, the conflict is between science and any authority who would "inhibit scientific development," with Christianity singled out for opposing theories of evolving species and a moving earth.

Given the shrill tone of the ongoing American controversy over teaching evolution in public schools and the rising influence of both secular scientism and biblical religion in modern America, the warfare metaphor remains alive and well. Growing public debates over stem-cell research, genetic engineering, human cloning, and global warming—debates in which the authority of science is often directly challenged by conservative Christians—further heighten the tension. For many scientists who feel embattled by biblical literalists, conflict remains the primary model for understanding the relationship between science and religion. Indeed, many partisans in these debates feel this way. Yet many scientists are drawn to religion and appreciate its historic contribution to society and culture.

Religious Beliefs of American Scientists

For an expression of the complex tension between science and religion in the American scientific mind, we need look no further than one of the icons of the twentieth century. A stone's throw from the Potomac River in Washington, D.C., a bronze statue of Albert Einstein reposes in a garden beside the National Academy of Sciences. Could a more fitting individual symbolize the highest echelon of scientists in America? Having fled to the United States from the secular horrors of Nazi Germany because of his religious heritage, Einstein never ceased musing about religion and once challenged quantum uncertainty by famously denying that God plays dice with the universe. Late in life, however, in his 1939 address, "Science and Religion," at Princeton Theological School, he concluded, "In their struggle for the ethical good, teachers of religion must have the stature to give up the doctrine of a personal God, that is, give up that source of fear and hope which in the past placed such vast power in the hands of priests."

His own struggle over the relationship between science and religion raises the broader question: What do American scientists hope and believe regarding religion? An early pioneer who sought to answer that question was Bryn Mawr psychologist James H. Leuba. In 1914 and again in 1933 Leuba surveyed American biological and physical scientists on their views regarding what he described as "the two central beliefs of the Christian religion": a God influenced by worship, and an afterlife. He maintained that without these "fundamental dogmas" Christianity could not survive. Inquiring about these beliefs among scientists was appropriate, he asserted, because scientists "enjoy great influence in the modern world, even in matters religious." He divided his respondents among rank-and-file bench scientists and the so-called greater scientists.

To see if scientists' beliefs had changed since his day, I joined journalist Larry Witham during the late 1990s to ask American scientists Leuba's two questions again: Do you believe in (1) "a God in intellectual and affective communication with humankind . . . to whom one may pray in expectation of receiving an answer" and (2) "personal immortality." Yes, no, and don't know (or agnostic) were the only options offered.

Responses were strictly anonymous. Our polling closely tracked Leuba's methods. First we surveyed a random sample of biological and physical scientists (the latter included mathematicians) listed in the standard reference work *American Men and Women of Science*, just as Leuba did in 1914 (*and Women* was added years after Leuba's surveys). Leuba's second quarry, "greater scientists," was based on a random sample of persons so designated by stars next to their listings. That distinction is no longer made in *American Men and Women of Science*, so we fell back on the much more-elite membership rolls of the National Academy of Sciences (NAS), whose core biological and physical science sections we surveyed in their entirety. By survey response standards, the two questions touched a nerve then and now, and better than half of those polled responded each time.

The 40 Percent Solution

One number resonates through more than eight decades: 40 percent. Four in ten of Leuba's scientists believed in God as defined in his survey. The same is true today. Somewhat more, about 50 percent, held to faith in an afterlife in Leuba's day, but now that figure is also 40 percent. Thus, one of Leuba's predictions, which Witham and I call his "general theory of disbelief," failed. Progress in science, Leuba wrote around 1914, would demand "a revision of public opinion regarding ... the two cardinal beliefs of official Christianity." He expected religious belief to wane among both American scientists and Americans in general. But scientists today no more jettison Christianity's "two cardinal beliefs" than their counterparts did in 1914. Gallup surveys suggest the same for the general population.

The second part of Leuba's survey—a poll of the scientific elite—found much higher levels of disbelief and doubt. In 1914 fewer than one in three of Leuba's "greater" scientists expressed belief in God, and only a slightly larger fraction in immortality. In 1933 more than 80 percent of the top natural scientists rejected both cardinal beliefs of traditional Christianity. Witham and I call Leuba's second hypothesis his "special theory of disbelief." The "greater" scientists are less accepting of the supernatural than are "lesser" scientists, Leuba postulated, because of their "superior knowledge, understanding, and experience." The NAS members provide a perhaps more-immaculate sample of the elite than Leuba's starred entries did. Congress created the National Academy of Sciences in 1863, and after naming its first members, Congress empowered them and their successors to choose all later members. Its current membership of eighteen hundred remains the closest thing to peerage in American science. Their responses validate Leuba's speculation about the beliefs of topflight scientists. Disbelief among NAS members responding to our survey exceeded 90 percent. Of course, the increase among topflight scientists may be less chronological and more a reflection that our survey responders were pulled from a more-elite sample than Leuba's "greater" scientists, but this interpretation would still please Leuba. NAS biologists are the most skeptical, with 95 percent of our respondents evincing atheism or agnosticism. Mathematicians in the NAS are more accepting: One in six expressed belief in a personal God.

Pyramid of Disbelief

What stands out from our survey data is that, in terms of its relationship to religion, American science did not change fundamentally during the twentieth century. Measured by religious belief, professional science is like a pyramid. At the top is acute disbelief. Scientists in the middle are significantly less believing—by more than half—than citizens in general, while the wide and heavy base is more firmly sunk into its religious surroundings. Of course, this finding strikes many people as simply confirming the obvious. A general sense exists that individuals with higher educational attainment or material success tend to be less religious. Further, some risk lies in sorting scientists into a professional hierarchy, as if stars after their listing in *American Men of Science* or NAS membership inevitably determines who the "greater" scientists are. Yet the acceptance of such distinctions within the scientific community suggests that the hierarchy must have some value, at least to the scientists themselves.

The question remains, however: Are the deepest contemporary scientific minds drawn to atheism, or does elite scientific society itself select for the trait of disbelief? The answer seems to be a bit of both, says philosopher of science Michael Rose, who has made a career of studying how biologists do their work. As an early member of the modern historical school of science, Ruse cannot but see social factors influencing both disbelief among biologists and membership selection within the NAS. Overtly religious members would doubtless feel tension, especially if their beliefs were theologically conservative.

Legendary evolutionary biologist Ernst Mayr, an NAS member since 1954, made a study of disbelief among his Harvard University colleagues in the National Academy of Sciences. "It turned out we were all atheists," he recalled in an interview. "I found that there were two sources." One Mayr typified as, "Oh, I became an atheist very early. I just couldn't believe all that supernatural stuff." But others told him, "I just couldn't believe that there could be a God with all this evil in the world." Mayr noted, "Most atheists combine the two. This combination makes it impossible to believe in God."

It is with some irony, then, that the NAS, like many scientific organizations, serves and lives off a much more staunchly believing public. The academy's primary work is to produce on average one technical report a day to advise members of Congress and other government officials, lobby for research funds, and promote good science. Although the NAS is mindful of its obligation to support the commonweal, it can be a delicate course to maneuver. Disbelief and belief have often become a major public relations issue for science in religious America.

"I asked some people at the NAS why they don't have a

section on evolution," said William B. Provine, an evolutionist and science historian at Cornell University, in an interview. The answer: "Too controversial." Yet, in 1998 the NAS issued a report proudly promoting the teaching of evolution in public school. "Whether God exists or not is a question about which science is neutral," the report cautiously begins, before launching its scientific arguments against religious objections to teaching evolution. The irony is striking: A group of specialists who are nearly all nonbelievers tell the public that "science is neutral" on the God question.

Such is the balancing act that materialists in science must play, living and working as they do in a traditionally Christian culture. Matt Cartmill, president of the American Association of Physical Anthropologists, noted in an interview, "Many scientists are atheists or agnostics who want to believe that the natural world they study is all there is, and being only human, they try to persuade themselves that science gives them the grounds for that belief. It's an honorable belief, but it isn't a research finding." Some scientists try to make it so, however. At a 1997 symposium, for example, the Society for Neuroscience heard about the "God module," a spot in the brain that apparently produces religious feelings. The report made front-page news across the country and excited widespread comment. Evidence for the report came from research on patients with temporal lobe epilepsy, many of whom have religious experiences during their seizures. This, as well as other research in neurobiology, which is finally beginning to unravel the mysteries of the human brain, threatens to drive the human soul out of its last physical refuge. The report inevitably drew critical comment from some conservative Christians. "You may be sure that scientific materialists will never discover a 'materialist module,' meaning a brain part that causes people to fantasize that they can explain the mind in strictly materialist terms," antievolution leader Phillip Johnson wryly observed.

Looking for areas of cooperation, secular scientists and mainstream religious leaders have found a modicum of common ground in concern for the environment. Carl Sagan broke the ice between the camps with his 1990 open letter welcoming and challenging the religious community to get on board with the movement to save the planet. The next year Sagan stood beside a robed Episcopal bishop in Manhattan's Cathedral of St. John the Divine as they cochaired the joint appeal by science and religion for the environment.

A similar alliance drew people from the two groups together at the American Museum of Natural History in New York City in 1998. One paleontologist at the museum, the noted evolutionist Niles Eldredge, said the meeting was all to the good. For those wary of public relations debacles, the friendly focus on ecology can easily obscure the troublesome God question. "There's an ecological component to all concepts of God," Eldredge said. He was quick to add, however, that the environment may be the only thing science and religion can civilly discuss.

Lutheran theologian Philip Hefner is no fan of Fundamentalists and sees himself as proscience. His journal *Zygon*
is dedicated to linking science and faith while avoiding the
extremes of either camp. As a student of theologian Paul Tillich, however, Hefner is on personal terms with symbols and
myths. Myths can overpower at times, he says, and science
is at fault as much as religion. Sadly for America, its greatest myth about science and religion is a legal melodrama, the
1925 John Scopes "monkey" trial. This myth has clung te-
naciously to American intellectual life ever since, precisely
because it supports the historical "conflict" model for understanding the relationship between science and religion. Indeed, *Scopes* has become America's Galileo. "The myth is that
scientists are courageous loners who are willing to die for the
truth," Hefner explained in an interview. "Organized religion
is *ipso facto* opposed to intellectual freedom and the freedom
of truth. Organized religion is the enemy. When heave comes
to shove, organized religion will kill the courageous scientist.
But you'll never get that across." Legend trumps history every time, especially when it reinforces our presumptions.

APPENDIX

Historical Surveys of the Religious
Beliefs of American Scientists

Sociologist James H. Leuba pioneered the study of the religious beliefs of American scientists. In 1914 and 1933, Leuba surveyed the beliefs of American scientists on what he deemed the two key questions of theism: belief in a personal God and belief in an afterlife. He sent a brief survey instrument to a representative sample of the scientists listed in the book *American Men of Science*. At the time, this reference work indicated "greater" scientists with stars next to their names. Leuba published the responses both of the group as a whole and of the starred scientists alone. His surveys became classics in the field. As such, they attracted the attention of journalist Larry A. Witham and me. During a 1995 interview in which Witham asked me about them, I suggested that we redo Leuba's surveys. As a result of this suggestion, in 1996 and 1998, we conducted surveys of American scientists that followed Leuba's techniques as nearly as possible, including the wording of the survey instrument. The reference work used by Leuba, now called *American Men and Women of Science*, no longer distinguishes between "greater" and "lesser" scientists, so instead we surveyed members of the National Academy of Sciences as our "greater" scientists. This appendix reprints the text of our survey instrument and the published results of the various surveys.

In addition to dividing his survey findings between "greater" scientists and scientists as a whole, Leuba also divided his findings between biological and physical scientists. He defined the former group as all scientists "concerned with living matter." He defined the latter group as those "concerned with inanimate matter," including physicists, chemists, astronomers, and, in 1914 but not in 1933, mathematicians. For consistency with the benchmark 1914 survey, we included mathematicians in our sample of physical scientists.

Survey Instrument
A STATISTICAL INQUIRY

*(A survey of American scientists first taken
by Professor James Leuba in 1916)*

Conflicting statements are confidently made regarding [whether scientists hold a] belief in God and personal immortality. Nevertheless, sufficient data are not extant to support any supposition.

The accompanying questions are sent to 1000 persons taken by chance from those listed in "American Men and Women of Science," in the hope of securing statistics valid for this group as a whole. The condition of success is that all those addressed respond. No satisfactory definite conclusions could be drawn if many of those addressed refuse or neglect to answer.

It will take you only a few seconds to make a mark by every statement true for you. Please do it, if at all possible, on receipt of this paper and return it in the enclosed stamped envelope.

A. CONCERNING THE BELIEF IN GOD.

❑ 1. I believe in a God in intellectual and affective communication with humankind, i.e., a God to whom one may pray in expectation of receiving an answer. By "answer" I mean more than the subjective, psychological effect of prayer.

❑ 2. I do not believe in a God as defined above.

❑ 3. I have no definite belief regarding this question (or I am an agnostic).

B. CONCERNING THE BELIEF IN PERSONAL IMMORTALITY, I.E., THE BELIEF IN CONTINUATION OF THE PERSON AFTER DEATH IN ANOTHER WORLD.

❑ 1. I believe in:

a. personal immortality for all people.

b. conditional immortality, i.e., for those who have reached a certain state of development.

❑ 2. I believe neither in conditional nor unconditional immortality of the person.

❑ 3. I have no definite belief regarding this question (or I am an agnostic).

Survey Results: Belief in God

ALL RESPONDENTS

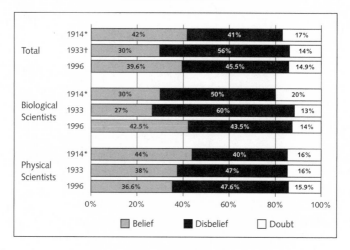

RESPONSES OF "GREATER" SCIENTISTS

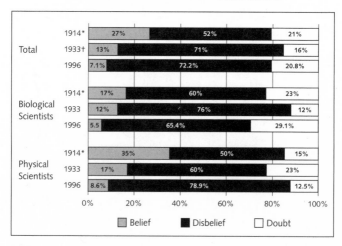

Survey Results: Belief in Immortality

ALL RESPONDENTS

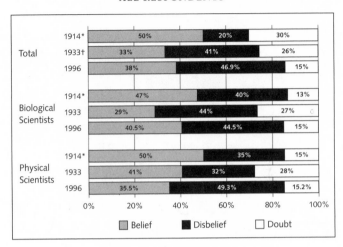

RESPONSES OF "GREATER" SCIENTISTS

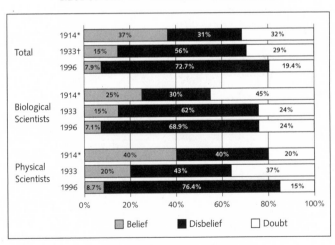

Appendix

NOTES

* All percentages provided for Leuba's surveys draw from his publications, with percentages rounded to the nearest whole number. For his 1914 survey, Leuba reported some of his information in pie charts without actual number entries attached for disbelief and doubt. Where no number is given in Leuba's publications, the numbers stated are estimated from his pie charts and available numbers in the text. Totals do not always equal 100 percent.

† Totals include the responses of sociologists and psychologists in addition to physical and biological scientists. Leuba reported responses for his 1933 survey only in a summary figure for all four groups.

SOURCES

The 1914 survey data appeared in James H. Leuba, *The Belief in God and Immortality: A Psychological, Anthropological and Statistical Study* (Boston: Sherman, French & Co., 1916), 221–81. The 1933 survey data appeared in James H. Leuba, "Religious Beliefs of American Scientists," *Harper's Magazine*, August 1934, 291–300. The 1996 survey data appeared in Edward J. Larson and Larry Witham, "Scientists Still Keeping the Faith," *Nature* 386 (1997), 435–36. The 1998 survey data appeared in Edward J. Larson and Larry Witham, "Leading Scientists Still Reject God," *Nature* 394 (1998), 313. Witham separately published data from our 1996 and 1998 surveys in Larry A. Witham, *Where Darwin Meets the Bible: Creationists and Evolutionists in America* (New York: Oxford University Press, 2002), 271–73. This appendix and Witham's 2002 book correct minor errors in our *Nature* articles.

INDEX

Index